Francis Frith's

South and West Somerset

Photographic Memories

Francis Frith's
South and West Somerset

Dennis and Jan Kelsall

First published in the United Kingdom in 2001 by
Frith Book Company Ltd

Paperback Edition 2001
ISBN 1-85937-318-6

British Library Cataloguing in Publication Data

Francis Frith's South and West Somerset
Dennis and Jan Kelsall

Frith Book Company Ltd
Frith's Barn, Teffont,
Salisbury, Wiltshire SP3 5QP
Tel: +44 (0) 1722 716 376
Email: info@francisfrith.co.uk
www.francisfrith.co.uk

Printed and bound in Great Britain

Front Cover: Chard, Cottages 1907 58768

Contents

Francis Frith: *Victorian Pioneer*

FRANCIS FRITH, Victorian founder of the world-famous photographic archive, was a complex and multi-talented man. A devout Quaker and a highly successful Victorian businessman, he was both philosophic by nature and pioneering in outlook.

By 1855 Francis Frith had already established a wholesale grocery business in Liverpool, and sold it for the astonishing sum of £200,000, which is the equivalent today of over £15,000,000. Now a multi-millionaire, he was able to indulge his passion for travel. As a child he had pored over travel books written by early explorers, and his fancy and imagination had been stirred by family holidays to the sublime mountain regions of Wales and Scotland. 'What a land of spirit-stirring and enriching scenes and places!' he had written. He was to return to these scenes of grandeur in later years to 'recapture the thousands of vivid and tender memories', but with a different purpose. Now in his thirties, and captivated by the new science of photography, Frith set out on a series of pioneering journeys to the Nile regions that occupied him from 1856 until 1860.

Intrigue and Adventure

He took with him on his travels a specially-designed wicker carriage that acted as both dark-room and sleeping chamber. These far-flung journeys were packed with intrigue and adventure. In his life story, written when he was sixty-three, Frith tells of being held captive by bandits, and of fighting 'an awful midnight battle to the very point of surrender with a deadly pack of hungry, wild dogs'. Sporting flowing Arab costume, Frith arrived at Akaba by camel seventy years before Lawrence, where he encountered 'desert princes and rival sheikhs, blazing with jewel-hilted swords'.

During these extraordinary adventures he was assiduously exploring the desert regions bordering the Nile and patiently recording the antiquities and peoples with his camera. He was the first photographer to venture beyond the sixth cataract. Africa was still the mysterious 'Dark Continent', and Stanley and Livingstone's historic meeting was a decade into the future. The conditions for picture taking confound belief. He laboured for hours in his wicker dark-room in the sweltering heat of the desert, while the volatile chemicals fizzed dangerously in their trays. Often he was forced to work in remote tombs and caves where conditions were cooler. Back in London he exhibited his photographs and was 'rapturously cheered' by members of the Royal Society. His reputation as a photographer was made overnight. An eminent modern historian has likened their impact on the population of the time to that on our own generation of the first photographs taken on the surface of the moon.

Venture of a Life-Time

Characteristically, Frith quickly spotted the opportunity to create a new business as a specialist publisher of photographs. He lived in an era of immense and sometimes violent change. For the poor in the early part of Victoria's reign work was a drudge and the hours long, and people had precious little free time to enjoy themselves. Most had no transport other than a cart or gig at their disposal, and had not travelled far beyond the boundaries of their own town or village. However,

by the 1870s, the railways had threaded their way across the country, and Bank Holidays and half-day Saturdays had been made obligatory by Act of Parliament. All of a sudden the ordinary working man and his family were able to enjoy days out and see a little more of the world.

With characteristic business acumen, Francis Frith foresaw that these new tourists would enjoy having souvenirs to commemorate their days out. In 1860 he married Mary Ann Rosling and set out with the intention of photographing every city, town and village in Britain. For the next thirty years he travelled the country by train and by pony and trap, producing fine photographs of seaside resorts and beauty spots that were keenly bought by millions of Victorians. These prints were painstakingly pasted into family albums and pored over during the dark nights of winter, rekindling precious memories of summer excursions.

The Rise of Frith & Co

Frith's studio was soon supplying retail shops all over the country. To meet the demand he gathered about him a small team of photographers, and published the work of independent artist-photographers of the calibre of Roger Fenton and Francis Bedford. In order to gain some understanding of the scale of Frith's business one only has to look at the catalogue issued by Frith & Co in 1886: it runs to some 670 pages, listing not only many thousands of views of the British Isles but also many photographs of most European countries, and China, Japan, the USA and Canada – note the sample page shown above from the hand-written *Frith & Co* ledgers detailing pictures taken. By 1890 Frith had created the greatest specialist photographic publishing company in the world,

Frith's death, a new card measuring 5.5 x 3.5 inches became the standard format, but it was not until 1902 that the divided back came into being, with address and message on one face and a full-size illustration on the other. *Frith & Co* were in the vanguard of postcard development, and Frith's sons Eustace and Cyril continued their father's monumental task, expanding the number of views offered to the public and recording more and more places in Britain, as the coasts and countryside were opened up to mass travel.

Francis Frith died in 1898 at his villa in Cannes, his great project still growing. The archive he created continued in business for another seventy years. By 1970 it contained over a third of a million pictures of 7,000 cities, towns and villages. The massive photographic record Frith has left to us stands as a living monument to a special and very remarkable man.

with over 2,000 outlets – more than the combined number that Boots and W H Smith have today! The picture on the right shows the *Frith & Co* display board at Ingleton in the Yorkshire Dales. Beautifully constructed with mahogany frame and gilt inserts, it could display up to a dozen local scenes.

Postcard Bonanza

The ever-popular holiday postcard we know today took many years to develop. In 1870 the Post Office issued the first plain cards, with a pre-printed stamp on one face. In 1894 they allowed other publishers' cards to be sent through the mail with an attached adhesive halfpenny stamp. Demand grew rapidly, and in 1895 a new size of postcard was permitted called the court card, but there was little room for illustration. In 1899, a year after

Frith's Archive: *A Unique Legacy*

FRANCIS FRITH'S legacy to us today is of immense significance and value, for the magnificent archive of evocative photographs he created provides a unique record of change in 7,000 cities, towns and villages throughout Britain over a century and more. Frith and his fellow studio photographers revisited locations many times down the years to update their views, compiling for us an enthralling and colourful pageant of British life and character.

We tend to think of Frith's sepia views of Britain as nostalgic, for most of us use them to conjure up memories of places in our own lives with which we have family associations. It often makes us forget that to Francis Frith they were records of daily life as it was actually being lived in the cities, towns and villages of his day. The Victorian age was one of great and often bewildering change for ordinary people, and though the pictures evoke an impression of slower times, life was as busy and hectic as it is today.

We are fortunate that Frith was a photographer of the people, dedicated to recording the minutiae of everyday life. For it is this sheer wealth of visual data, the painstaking chronicle of changes in dress, transport, street layouts, buildings, housing, engineering and landscape that captivates us so much today. His remarkable images offer us a powerful link with the past and with the lives of our ancestors.

Today's Technology

Computers have now made it possible for Frith's many thousands of images to be accessed almost instantly. In the Frith archive today, each photograph is carefully 'digitised' then stored on a CD Rom. Frith archivists can locate a single photograph amongst thousands within seconds. Views can be catalogued and sorted under a variety of categories of place and content to the immediate benefit of researchers.

Inexpensive reference prints can be created for them at the touch of a mouse button, and a wide range of books and other printed materials assembled and published for a wider, more general readership - in the next twelve months over a hundred Frith local history titles will be published! The day-to-day workings of the archive are very different from how they were in Francis Frith's time: imagine the herculean task of sorting through eleven tons of glass negatives as Frith had to do to locate a particular sequence of pictures! Yet

See Frith at www.francisfrith.co.uk

the archive still prides itself on maintaining the same high standards of excellence laid down by Francis Frith, including the painstaking cataloguing and indexing of every view.

It is curious to reflect on how the internet now allows researchers in America and elsewhere greater instant access to the archive than Frith himself ever enjoyed. Many thousands of individual views can be called up on screen within seconds on one of the Frith internet sites, enabling people living continents away to revisit the streets of their ancestral home town, or view places in Britain where they have enjoyed holidays. Many overseas researchers welcome the chance to view special theme selections, such as transport, sports, costume and ancient monuments.

We are certain that Francis Frith would have heartily approved of these modern developments in imaging techniques, for he himself was always working at the very limits of Victorian photographic technology.

The Value of the Archive Today

Because of the benefits brought by the computer, Frith's images are increasingly studied by social historians, by researchers into genealogy and ancestory, by architects, town planners, and by teachers and schoolchildren involved in local history projects.

In addition, the archive offers every one of us an opportunity to examine the places where we and our families have lived and worked down the years. Highly successful in Frith's own era, the archive is now, a century and more on, entering a new phase of popularity.

The Past in Tune with the Future

Historians consider the Francis Frith Collection to be of prime national importance. It is the only archive of its kind remaining in private ownership and has been valued at a million pounds. However, this figure is now rapidly increasing as digital technology enables more and more people around the world to enjoy its benefits.

Francis Frith's archive is now housed in an historic timber barn in the beautiful village of Teffont in Wiltshire. Its founder would not recognize the archive office as it is today. In place of the many thousands of dusty boxes containing glass plate negatives and an all-pervading odour of photographic chemicals, there are now ranks of computer screens. He would be amazed to watch his images travelling round the world at unimaginable speeds through network and internet lines.

The archive's future is both bright and exciting. Francis Frith, with his unshakeable belief in making photographs available to the greatest number of people, would undoubtedly approve of what is being done today with his lifetime's work. His photographs, depicting our shared past, are now bringing pleasure and enlightenment to millions around the world a century and more after his death.

South and West Somerset
- *An Introduction*

Even in the days before the motorway was constructed, Somerset was often ignored by the thousands of holidaymakers who passed through each year, intent on the more popular coasts, resorts and villages that lie further to the west. Yet anyone who devotes a little time to its exploration cannot fail to be impressed by the immense variety that exists in its small towns, villages and countryside. Situated between the gentle heartland of England and the western extremities of its Atlantic peninsula, Somerset reflects something of each, whilst at the same time expressing its own distinctive character, subtly different from anything to be found elsewhere in the country.

The importance and loveliness of its natural attributes have been recognised in the designation of Exmoor as a National Park and the Mendip, Quantock and Blackdown Hills as Areas of Outstanding Natural Beauty. But many other areas of the county, such as the Vale of Taunton, Hamdon Hill and the Levels, have their own particular charm and significance too. The diversity and beauty of the landscape is not, however, entirely due to nature,

but has been influenced over the millennia by the hand of man, which has moulded the different environments to best serve his purpose. But, though the changes have been profound - predominantly, the replacement of primeval forest by open cultivation and grazing and the draining of huge areas that were neither sea nor land - they have generally been such as to allow nature to adapt in pleasing response.

The character of the land is revealed not only in distant views, but also in the churches, old houses and other buildings that dot the landscape. The rocks that lie beneath its verdant cloak change abruptly throughout the length of the county and each has its own distinctive colour and texture. The light grey limestones found in the north, the golden tints of Hamdon and the sandstones of Exmoor each find a different expression in the local architecture.

Somerset is also a land of history, and almost everywhere has a tale to tell, from the mysteries of prehistoric ritual to happenings of our own generation, some of which have left visible signs upon the land. Although less impressive than that at Stonehenge, there is an enigmatic stone circle from the Bronze Age by the road on a hill south-west of Porlock. Many of the hilltops of Exmoor, the Brendons and the Quantocks have the remains of ancient burial sites or defensive enclosures, which were built over a period of some two-and-a-half

millennia before the arrival of the Romans. Indeed, some were still in use when the Fosse Way was being built, that marvellous statement of engineering and organisational ability which dissects the county in its 210-mile course across England between Axminster and Lincoln. Only scant evidence of any Saxon constructions remains, but many of today's villages were established during this period, several being sufficiently important to have their own mint. A settlement's name is often a clue to its origins.

It is in and around the smaller towns and villages that many of the surviving buildings from the medieval and later periods can be found, notably in their churches, manor houses, municipal buildings and old, picturesque cottages. However, it is lamentable to note that many fine and characterful structures in the larger towns, which were still standing until relatively recently, have been demolished, discarded in the name of progress, often to make way for monotonous high street shopping developments. It would be interesting to know how many of these will be considered worthy of preservation to delight future generations.

The county has been the stage for some of England's momentous episodes, when the course of history was set by the turn of events here. It was on the Athelney marshes, not far from Langport, where King Alfred of Wessex burnt the cakes, his mind preoccupied with the defence of his kingdom against the Viking Great Army, which had plagued

the country throughout his reign. From here he raised an army which met the invading forces at Edington, just over the border in Wiltshire, and in the ensuing battle gained a decisive victory. In the peace treaty that followed, Guthrum, the defeated leader of the Scandinavians, agreed to withdraw from Wessex and renounce his pagan faith in favour of Christianity.

Eight centuries later, James Scott, the first Duke of Monmouth, was less fortunate when he returned from exile in the Netherlands to contest his uncle's accession to the throne. The illegitimate son of Charles I, his sympathies lay with the Protestant cause, and in June 1685, following the death of Charles II, he landed at Lyme Regis with a small band of eighty-two supporters. He marched north, swelling his forces along the way from the farmers and labourers who worked the land. After taking Taunton, he was proclaimed king, but failed to gain the all-important backing of the gentry; his march north was foiled when he was unable to take Bristol. He returned to Bridgwater, only to find the royal army encamped on the marshes at Westonzoyland. Disillusioned, some of his followers deserted, but on 6 July Monmouth decided to launch a night attack. His strategy almost paid off, but he missed finding the safe crossing point at the final ditch separating him from his goal. Having then lost the element of surprise, his untrained army was cut down. Monmouth was captured

shortly afterwards and beheaded only days later on Tower Hill after an unsuccessful plea for clemency to James II. In the ruthless Bloody Assizes that followed, the Lord Chief Justice, George Jeffreys, was no less forgiving, and more that six hundred of Monmouth's followers were either transported or condemned to a horrible death.

That same strong sense of belief in a cause and determination to make a difference is displayed in the Somerset men and women whose names and deeds have entered the history books. Amongst them is Robert Blake, a merchant's son from Bridgwater, who, after entering parliament at the age of forty gave his support to Cromwell's cause during the Civil Wars. His outstanding military career and promotion to admiral was not equalled until Nelson's command of the Navy. Born half a century later in 1652 at East Coker was William Dampier; despite spending part of his career as a pirate, he is considered one of the greatest seamen of his time. He circumnavigated the globe three times and led several expeditions of scientific discovery. Dampier's meticulous observation and record of the oceans, their weather and the places he visited produced a body of information that Nelson still found valuable a hundred years later. In our own era too, Somerset has produced a number of notable people. Ernest Bevin, the great trades unionist and labour minister, was born in Winsford and the first woman cabinet member and

chairman of the TUC, Margaret Grace Bondfield, came from Chard.

To a greater or lesser extent, the nature of the land has moulded the course of the lives of the people who have been born and lived there, and its atmospheric beauty has also been a source of inspiration for great literature. The 19th-century Richard Doddridge Blackmore set his best-remembered novel, 'Lorna Doone', amongst the turbulent wilds of Exmoor, where his grandfather had been a country parson. Samuel Taylor Coleridge and the Wordsworths, Dorothy and William, spent time in and around the Quantock Hills, and their devotees still come to search out the places that stimulated their emotions - such as Watchet, a supposed setting in 'The Rime of the Ancient Mariner'.

Many of the scenes captured by the photographs in this book have associations with the events and people that have contributed to Somerset's story, but others hold interest in their own right, as a more commonplace record of places and daily events in the lives of ordinary people. Whilst for centuries artists' images have represented the world and society in which they lived, it has only been since the advent of the camera in the late 19th century that the sparkling elements of im-mediacy, spontaneity and informality have actually been captured. True, the camera might lie and compositions may well be artificially posed, but as the photographs here demonstrate, it shows how our world is changing in a way that no other medium can.

The photographs in this book span a period from the end of the 19th to the middle of the 20th centuries, and present a vivid picture of a period which, although still within living or anecdotal memories, is rapidly becoming history. For those who know the county, they will stir memories and provoke discussion on the way that things have changed. These images may encourage others to visit the towns, villages and countryside of Somerset, not just as tourists passing through, but in a more leisurely exploration to discover what lies beneath the surface.

This is one of two volumes devoted to the county, each of which covers about half Somerset's geographical area. In the first volume, the northern boundaries were returned to their traditional lines, to reclaim Bath and those delightful towns and villages that speckle the countryside north of the Mendip Hills. A more arbitrary split has been chosen to divide the county into two, roughly following a line southeast from the estuary of the River Parrett. This represents merely an editorial convenience, with no intention to compartmen-talise the county, and which we hope will not arouse the passions that the imposition of Avon did, a quarter of a century ago.

Exmoor and its Fringes

Selworthy, The Village 1923 75020
Taken from below the late 14th-century Church of All Saints, this photograph looks past the war memorial to the cottages of the village. At one time, the external walls of many of the churches in the area were coated with a weatherproofing mixture of lime and tallow, but only at Selworthy is this practice maintained.

▼ **Selworthy, The Almshouses 1900** 45701

The village is part of the Holnicote Estate, the gift of the Acland family to the National Trust, to which many of the village's thatched cottages now belong - their preservation is thus assured. It was once believed that Sir Thomas Acland built the cottages in 1828, but it has recently been discovered that they were adapted from medieval farmhouses already standing.

▼ **Selworthy, The Village 1890** 23528

An old woman sits below this ancient creeper-clad tree, whilst another poses for the cameraman outside her cottage porch. Notice the semi-circular oven protruding from the wall beside the chimney, a feature of many period cottages in the area. It was used to bake bread, then very much a staple of the diet.

▲ **Allerford, The Corner 1923** 75023

This attractive village lies just off the main road, where children sit beside the bus stop. The Blue Bus Company operated services in the area from 1916 until 1946. Behind is Cross Lane House, which was a working farm until 1968 and is now run as a restaurant and hotel.

◀ **Allerford,
The Bridge 1900** 45703
Looking down towards
the village, this photograph
shows the ford that gave
Allerford its name; beside
it stands an ancient, two-
arched packhorse bridge.
Nearby, the thatched
former schoolhouse is now
home to the West Somerset
Museum of Rural Life,
which gives a fascinating
insight into the daily lives
of people in the area not
that long ago.

◀ **Porlock**
High Street 1919 69270
This photograph was taken outside the 13th-century church of St Dubricius, and shows Isaac Burgess standing beside a horse and trap outside his bakery. The family firm continued in business until 1983, when it sold out to Stenner's. They owned the greengrocer's shop next door, and having amalgamated the two premises, continue as the village bakers.

Bossington, The Village 1931

84861

Lying near the coast below Bossington Hill, these cottages overlook a stream that once powered a corn mill. Close by is Lynch Chapel, a medieval chapel-of-ease to the church at Selworthy. With the manor, it formerly belonged to the abbey at Athelney, but it fell into disuse after the Dissolution until Sir Thomas Acland restored it in the 19th century.

Porlock, The Ship Inn 1890   23509

Standing at the bottom of the notoriously steep climb of Porlock Hill, the Ship Inn appears little changed today, despite the removal of its attractive wooden porches. It was supposedly here that the prolific writer, Robert Southey, a close friend of Coleridge and poet laureate from 1807, composed his verse on Porlock's 'verdant vale'.

Porlock, On the Road to Hawkcombe 1890

23530

The lane, still a woodland track higher up, leads from Porlock Church into Hawk Combe. Hawkcombe and Whitehall Cottages are there today, but a bridge now replaces the ford where the child and dog are standing. In 1891, to the left beyond the cottages, a new cemetery for the village was opened on land that actually belonged to Luccombe parish.

▼ Porlock, The Weir 1907 58365

At one time the sea extended to Porlock itself, but a retreating shoreline has left it a mile inland and the harbour is now here, at Porlock Weir. The small white building behind the harbour towards the left is the Ship Inn, which dates at least from 1651. The Anchor Hotel occupies the more recent buildings to the right.

▼ Porlock, The Weir 1929 82188

The place was once a thriving fishing port and was busy with coastal trade from Wales, bringing coal and limestone and exporting woodland products in return. The harbour was improved in the 19th century by the addition of lock gates, which allowed cargoes to be handled at all stages of the tide.

▲ Culbone, Church Combe 1929

82193

The tiny church of St Beuno is cupped in a sylvan cleft that runs steeply to the sea. The church measures only 35 feet long by 12 feet 4 inches wide, and has the distinction of being the smallest complete parish church in England. The woodland provided a living for the villagers, who coppiced the oaks for tanbark, charcoal and timbers.

◀ **Oare,**
The Vale c1960 03003
John Blackmore was rector of St Mary the Virgin, and it was here that his grandson Richard set the scene for the tragic marriage ceremony of Lorna Doone to John Ridd in his famous novel. The tale is woven around both fact and local folklore and takes place during the period of the Monmouth Rebellion.

◀ **Luccombe, Cottages 1890** 23527
Beyond the cottages stands the village school, which served the community between 1881 and 1946. The schoolmistress lived in a cottage, which now replaces the one where a man here sits on the step. The tall chimney next door rises above a bread oven, whose rounded shape protrudes from the wall of the house.

◄ **Horner,**
The Village 1923 75012
A girl leans idly against a wall beside a creeper-covered cottage, a scene that has not greatly changed in the seventy years that have passed since the photograph was taken. Teas are now served at the cottage during the summer months, and the ancient woodland which cloaks the surrounding slopes is a popular choice for walkers and horse-riders.

▼ **Luccombe, On Horner**
Water 1901 47390
Horner Water winds through a steep, densely-wooded vale, which lies below the abrupt northern slopes of Dunkery Hill, Somerset's highest point. Here, it passes beneath an old packhorse bridge beside what is now a caravan site at Burrowhayes Farm.

◄ **Timberscombe**
The Village c1955
T335012
The Lion Inn developed as a hostelry serving coaches travelling the road between Minehead and Tiverton and dates from the 15th century. The Coombe Stores and adjacent shop served the village's needs, and judging from the variety of notices in the windows and on the board outside, were a main source of local information.

Wheddon Cross, The Rest and Be Thankful Hotel c1950 W597006
Situated beside the coach road between Minehead and Exeter, at the top of a high ridge dividing the Avill and Quarme Rivers, the Rest and be Thankful Hotel was aptly named. Thomas Crockford, a local landowner, built it around 1825, adding stabling so that horses could be changed after the climb. It still provides hospitality to today's travellers.

Exford, The White Horse Hotel 1940 89008
Originally a 17th-century building, the White Horse Hotel developed as a coaching inn and had extensive stabling. During a terrible flood in 1952, the river burst its banks and five feet of water surged through the hotel and stables. Luckily, the horses were freed as the stables collapsed, and next morning all twenty-two were found alive and well.

Exford,
The Bridge 1892 31193
Exford was a centre for stag hunting, and provided kennels and stables for the Devon and Somerset Hunt. The bridge, which replaced an earlier timber structure, carries the main route onto the moor, but at one time travellers had to ford the Exe. Children pose for the photographer by the parapet, an experience probably remembered for some time.

**Exford,
The Smithy c1920**
E50501
This fascinating photograph shows the village smithy at work, the horse waiting patiently for the task to be finished. A large grinding wheel stands to the side, and the open door is plastered with handbills. Although the forge and chimney were built of stone, the workshed is constructed of rough-cut logs and thatch, and fire must have been an ever-present risk.

Simonsbath, The Village 1907 59429
Simonsbath has the distinction of being Somerset's most westerly village. It lies in a wooded vale below desolate moorland, the source of the River Barle. Here, looking across the valley to the northeast, we can see the 19th-century St Luke's Church; in the centre, at the bottom of the valley, is the Exmoor Forest Hotel.

◄ **Exford,
The Village 1940** 89011
Along the road at the edge
of the village, this row of
buildings overlooks an
open green. The nearer of
the two shops was then the
post office, and next door is
Moore's family grocer and
draper. Today Exford is
regarded by many as the
'capital' of Exmoor, and it is a
popular centre for walkers.

▼ **Simonsbath, The Exmoor
Forest Hotel 1907** 59434
For some eight centuries
after the Normans arrived in
England, Exmoor was a royal
hunting forest, although
there is little record that
kings ever came to take
advantage of their privileges.
However, the village
developed around a hunting
lodge and served as a base
from which to administer the
forest laws.

◄ **Simonsbath,
The Post Office 1907** 59436
The Knight family acquired
the estate in the 19th century.
After enclosing areas of moorland, they attempted arable
farming and grazing. They also
discovered iron ore nearby,
but their mine was not profitable
and later closed. The post office
served the tiny community;
although telephones had still
to reach remote areas, it was
possible to send a telegram from
here.

Withypool, The Bridge c1960 W596039

The village, which nestles within a deep wooded fold of the moors, lays claim to having been the Norman capital of Fxmoor and was at the centre of a royal hunting forest. The six-arch bridge spans the River Barle; above the rooftops behind rises the square tower of St Andrew's Church, originally a chapel-of-ease to Hawkridge.

Winsford, The Royal Oak Inn 1930 83545

Originally a 13th-century farm, the building became a halt for packhorse trains carrying wool across the hills. Over time a hostelry developed, but only a hundred years ago, a dairy stood where the back bar is today. The Royal Oak's appearance has altered little in the last seventy years, and it continues to provide old-fashioned hospitality in a modern age.

Winsford, Blacksmith Bridge and the Church c1965 W112027
A blacksmith's forge used to stand beside this packhorse bridge spanning Winn Brook, one of eight bridges boasted by this tiny village. It was at Winsford that Ernest Bevin was born in 1881. He became General Secretary of the Transport and General Workers' Union and was later appointed Minister of Labour and then Foreign Secretary.

Dulverton, The River Barle 1934 86310
The River Barle appears here little more than a placid stream, but in 1953 a devastating flood swept through Dulverton from the hills above, inundating the bridge and destroying the cottages at the far end of the row. Since then, high parapets have been built along the riverbank to lessen the threat of future catastrophe.

**Dulverton,
The Lion Hotel 1896**
37653
On the edge of Exmoor
and with a fine river,
Dulverton became a
popular centre for
shooting and fishing:
at one time, there were
twenty hotels and inns
to cater for visitors.
Here, a coach is arriving
at the Lion Hotel and
the porter stands ready
at the door to receive
the new guests.

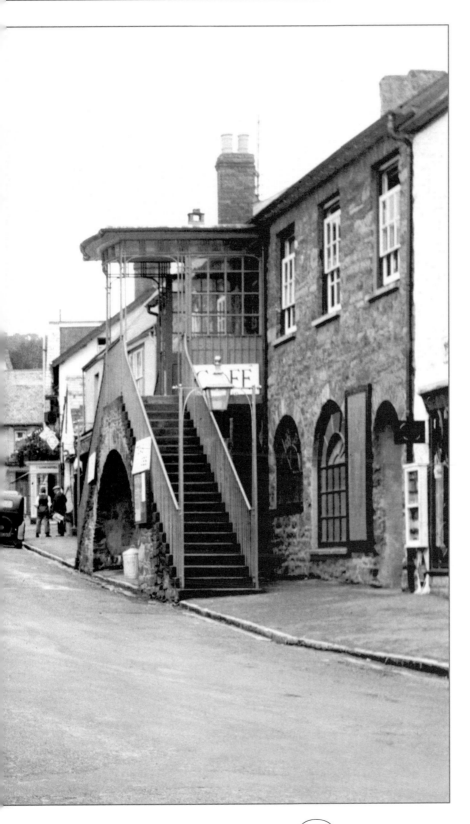

**Dulverton
Fore Street 1937**
88173
Sir Edwin Lutyens, whose work appears throughout Somerset, designed this curious external staircase and porch, which leads to the upper floor of Dulverton's Town Hall. The building was erected in 1866 and the new entrance was added during 1927. At the top of the street is All Saints' Church, founded in the 14th century by Augustinian monks from Barlynch Abbey.

The Coast and its Hinterland

Minehead
Churchtown 1888 20893
The town has increasingly succumbed to popularisation during the
last half-century, but some of the old buildings of Higher Town
below St Michael's Church have been preserved. Lining Church
Steps, these cottages are a fine illustration of vernacular domestic
architecture, a characteristic of which is a high chimney abutting
the street, often provided with a small 'lookout'.

Minehead, The Esplanade 1901 47366
Minehead had one of the coast's best harbours, and during the Middle Ages, it profited from trade and fishing. Although these declined during the late 18th century, the pleasant countryside and attractive seafront encouraged a growing holiday industry in its stead. Small traders and fishing boats, however, still used the harbour, some bringing coal to fuel the gasworks behind.

Minehead, Quay Street 1906 57164
Many of the cottages lining Quay Street, which leads below North Hill to the harbour, belonged to fishermen who once sailed after herring. But tourists encouraged new activities, and the end cottage became an agency for the Red Funnel Line, selling tickets for steamboat cruises. It also offered accommodation, as does, no doubt, the Red Lion opposite.

◀ **Minehead
The Promenade and
the Sands 1931** 84816
Despite the Council's
puritanical attitude to sea
bathing, there appear to be
plenty of people enjoying
the beach. But motorists
are perhaps getting a taste of
things to come, by having to
pay a toll to drive and park
along the eastern part of the
promenade. Today's scene
includes Butlin's Holiday
Camp in the background,
which opened in 1962.

◄ **Minehead, The Promenade 1919** 69237
In the early 20th century, Minehead was a genteel resort. With few frosts and plenty of fresh air, it became a fashionable wintering place, especially for convalescents and invalids. The Queen's Hall opened in 1914 with the London show 'Oh, I say', and in 1930, screened 'Disraeli', the first 'talkie' to be seen in Minehead.

▼ **Minehead, The Parade 1903** 49639
A well-laden coach and four arrive in the town, making its way towards the seafront and main hotels. It is passing the elaborate façade of the Market Hall, which had been completed only the year before, in 1902. Fourteen years after this photograph was taken, the science fiction writer Arthur C Clarke was born in nearby Blenheim Road.

◄ **Minehead The Esplanade Hotel 1923** 74988
Facing the sea and with a large garden and tennis court, this private hotel promoted itself as being central for the Staghound, Foxhound and Harrier Meets, popular sports for the gentry classes who then visited the town. It was converted into flats in the 1930s and more lately has been divided between a Baptist holiday centre and Foxes Hotel.

Minehead, The Plume of Feathers Hotel 1892 31224
Once known as the Middle Town Inn, the 17th-century Plume of Feathers was an old coaching establishment and, at one time, Minehead's largest hotel. It was demolished in 1966 and replaced by a retail block. However, Queen Anne's statue, which was moved from St Michael's Church to Wellington Square opposite the hotel in 1893, still stands there.

Dunster, Market House 1890 27512
The octagonal building standing in the centre of the high street was erected in 1609 as a market from which the famous locally-produced broadcloth was sold. Its builder, George Luttrell, owned Dunster Castle, which is now in the care of the National Trust. The tower on Conygar Hill was built in 1775 and gives a grand view across the bay.

Dunster, The Old Nunnery 1888 20919
Founded as a Benedictine house in 1090, Dunster priory fell into disuse after the Dissolution. However, several structures remain standing, including a great tithe barn and dovecote. Another survivor is this lovely tile-clad building, which was not in fact a nunnery, but more likely served as the guesthouse for visitors to the priory.

Dunster, The Dovecote and the Old Priory 1919 69262
The dovecote, where pigeons were bred as a ready source of meat throughout the year, is set amidst walled gardens. Behind is the church, which in 1498 was divided in half by a beautifully-carved screen to settle a dispute over its use between the parish and the monks. Today a road splits the gardens between the church and dovecote.

Carhampton, Sea Lane to Blue Anchor 1933 85931
Leaving the main road beside the church at Carhampton, a narrow track leads to the coast at Blue Anchor. The age of these cottages is not known, but a beam uncovered during recent restoration was found to be medieval. There used to be a forge at the back, and the curious dark triangular object has been identified as an anvil.

Blue Anchor, The Village 1936 87562
Taken from the Blue Anchor Hotel's balcony, this view looks across its garden to the promenade. In 1920, the industrialist 'Jack' Lysaght bought the estate; amongst other entertainments, he held open-air jazz concerts on the green. It is rumoured that the young princesses Elizabeth and Margaret once stayed at the summerhouse he built for his wife above the beach.

Blue Anchor, The Village 1935 87052
Flooding and erosion affect the coast, and the cliff edges to the east regularly crumble into the sea. In the 1890s, cottages along the seafront were washed away; to stem further damage, Lysaght constructed this sea wall and promenade in 1921. His efforts were effective, for they still provide an excellent walk along the front.

Blue Anchor, The Beach 1935 87048
Beyond the promenade, the bay sweeps around past Dunster to Minehead, which lies below the high promontory of North Hill. Then, as today, it was a popular spot for families, providing a more informal recreation than the nearby resort. Umbrellas provide shade from the sun, and a picnic basket suggests it might soon be time for lunch.

Old Cleeve, The Pillared Cottage 1930 83556
Two children sit outside the gateway to the aptly
named Pillar Cottage, where two massive masonry
pillars support an upper room to form a porch over
the doorway. The structure can be more clearly
seen if you pass by today, as creepers no longer
hide the walls.

Old Cleeve, The Village 1906 56810
A passing century has made little difference to this scene, which looks along a row of thatched cottages to St Andrew's Church in the centre of the village. Although the church was largely rebuilt in the 15th century, herringbone stonework is a characteristic of Norman architecture and there may have been a church here before William the Conqueror arrived.

Washford, The Village 1919 69281
Pictured from the junction with the main road, the lane leads down past the cottages towards the village school. Two men, one about to cycle away, stand outside the red stone cottages, which have attractively-patterned tiled roofs and fretwork bargeboards decorating the gable ends.

**Washford,
The Village 1930**
83511
At the other end of
the village, the road
on the left leads to
Cleeve Abbey.
Opposite the corner,
to the right of the
photograph, is
St Mary's Mission
Church. A ceremony
and procession led
by the Masonic Grand
Master of Somerset
accompanied the laying
of the foundation stone,
which took place in
1909.

▼ Washford, Cleeve Abbey Gateway 1935 86615

Although the church was destroyed after the Dissolution, many parts of this 13th-century Cistercian monastery survive and are now preserved by English Heritage. The gatehouse separated the community from the secular world and served the purpose of both entrance and a place where the poor could gather to receive alms. Over the inner doorway is a carving of the crucifixion.

▼ Watchet, St Decuman's Church 1923 75063

On the hill above Watchet stands a church to the 6th-century St Decuman. Whilst praying one day he was decapitated in an attack, but the saint afterwards took up his head and washed away the blood in a nearby holy well. The factory below is the Wansbrough Paper Mill, originally founded at Snailholt Farm in 1750 by the Wood family.

▲ Watchet, The Beach 1927 80604

Watchet's shingly beach has long been an attraction for children, who here search for curiosities along the tide line. Baggy knickers appear here to be the fashionable beachwear of the day, intended to preserve dignity, whilst at least allowing some freedom to paddle. The soft lias rocks of the cliffs are rich in fossils, and ammonites are commonly found.

◄ **Watchet, The Harbour Lighthouse 1923** 75062
Watchet's harbour used to be busy with commercial traffic, and to guide the boats in, the entrance is marked with a lighthouse. In 1900 a great storm hit the coast, severely damaging the harbour and hindering the shipping. The Urban District Council, which was created shortly afterwards, undertook the repairs at a cost of some £25,000.

**Watchet,
The Promenade 1906**
56796
The building at
the far end of the
promenade, opposite
Lee's Refreshment
Rooms, is the
Old Market Hall, which
now houses the town's
fascinating museum
and, above, the tiny
Holy Cross Chapel.
It also comprised the
lock-up for the court
leet, whose sessions
were held across the
road in the Bell Inn.

▼ **Watchet, The Harbour 1927** 80599

The repair works to the harbour have obviously been completed, with smart white-painted railings lining the quayside. However, this lad seems to share my opinion that you cannot see everything from where you are supposed to stand. The building on the far left housed the lifeboat station between 1875 and 1944, but is now the library.

▼ **Watchet, The Harbour 1927** 80597

The heavy-looking bales piled high on the quayside probably contain rags, and await loading onto the horse carts for delivery to the paper mill. Other cargoes to the port included grain from Ireland, which was taken for grinding at Stoate's flourmill in the town.

▲ **Watchet, The Harbour 1927**

80595

A major export from the town after 1855 was iron ore, which was mined in the Brendon Hills. It arrived at the harbour by rail for loading onto boats and transportation across the Bristol Channel to smelting furnaces in Newport. The trade came to an end in 1910, with the import of cheaper ore from Spain.

◄ **Williton,**
North Street 1929 82101
This smartly-dressed boy
has perhaps been sent
shopping, and drags his cart
in case the purchases are
too heavy. Both shops in
the photograph continue
in their original trades, the
bakery still being run by
the same Jones family,
whilst the butcher's shop
behind the boy has only
been in the hands of
two families since it
first opened.

Williton, Fore Street 1929 82133
The building next to the post office was formerly a stationer's and print shop, where Samuel Cox founded the West Somerset Free Press in 1860. At the rear, a non-conformist chapel, built in 1802, was subsequently outgrown by the congregation. It has since been used as a scout hut and postal sorting office before being converted into a private house.

◄ **East Quantoxhead 1929**
82153
Close to the Court House, an Elizabethan manor, lies this tranquil pond, constructed to hold water for a mill. The estate was granted to the Paganel family after the Conquest and, some two centuries later, passed in marriage to the Luttrells. It still belongs to the family, and thus has one of the longest recorded tenures in the country.

The Quantock Hills

◀ **East Quantoxhead, Townsend 1929** 82151
Townsend Farm overlooks a junction where the lane to East Quantoxhead leaves the main road. Only a mile from a pleasant and unspoilt beach, the area attracted holiday-makers, and the occupiers of Townsend House helped satisfy their needs by offering meals and accommodation. An interesting decorative panel on the wall between the upper windows is formed from beach pebbles.

◀ **East Quantoxhead, The Cliffs 1929** 82148
A path leads from the tiny village across the fields to low cliffs above this quiet beach. The thin strata of the rocks form attractive patterns in the headland, but they are soft and readily eroded by the sea. Embedded within the layers are numerous fossils: ammonites and gryphaea, sometimes called 'devil's toenails', are commonly found.

Holford, From the Firs 1897 40003
The last century has seen a considerable growth in the woodland that surrounds this tiny village, which nestles below the north-eastern corner of the Quantock Hills, and these Scots pines can still be found on the hill above. Bypassed by the main road, the village appears to have changed little, and many of the cottages retain their thatched roofs.

Holford, The Beeches 1897 40006
These fine trees still stand beside a lane near Holford's church. Native to this country, beeches were planted for shelter, ornament and, of course, their timber. Its close grain made it eminently suitable for a variety of turned objects, and its pliability was much exploited in the manufacture of chairs.

Holford, Alfoxton House 1903 50458
Spacious parkland surrounds Alfoxton House, which is now a comfortable hotel. William Wordsworth took the house for a year in 1797 and brought his sister, Dorothy, to live with him. She wrote about the place in her celebrated diary, and William composed several poems there. Coleridge, who then lived at nearby Nether Stowey, was a frequent visitor.

Dodington, The Hall 1929 82140
The house dates from 1591, and stands on the site of a pre-Norman manor held by Dodo, a royal forester under Edward the Confessor and from whom the village takes its name. By the 19th century the house had deteriorated, but Sir Thomas Acland, who preserved much of its surviving medieval decoration, restored it.

◀ **Nether Stowey
St Mary's Street 1929**
82113
The turnpike between
Bridgwater and Watchet
once ran along St Mary's
Street, and a tollhouse still
stands today. Between the
upper windows of the
building on the right is a fire
insurance plaque, which
signified that the owner had
paid for the services of the
fire brigade in the
unfortunate event of the
house catching fire.

◀ **Nether Stowey,
The Village 1895** 35764
Although many of the buildings are today little changed from those shown here, the lack of pavements and tarmac on the street gives it a vastly different appearance. The building occupied by Routley's Stores is Poole House, once the home of Thomas Poole. After inheriting his father's tannery business, he became literary patron to his friend Samuel Taylor Coleridge.

▼ **Nether Stowey,
The Post Office and
the Clock Tower 1929** 82138
The village lock-up and a medieval market cross and bell tower once stood here at the junction. The present tower was erected to commemorate Queen Victoria's silver jubilee in 1862 and carries the original town bell above the clock. Additions were made to celebrate Victoria's diamond jubilee and the Parish Council's centenary.

◀ **West Monkton
The Street c1955**
W602010
This view along the main street towards the church has little changed during fifty years. The post office stores continues to supply the needs of the village, and even the letterbox, advising that 'letters containing coin, paper money, or jewellery should not be posted in the box but registered', is still there.

Kingston St Mary, The Village c1960 K179008
The village claims fame in sharing its name with a cider apple. The view here looks along the main street towards the Swan Inn, which can just be discerned at the far end. The village shop on the left has now closed, but there is still an assortment of small metal advertising signs affixed to its wall.

Cothelstone, Cothelstone Lodge 1906 55780
On the northern slopes of Cothelstone Hill, Parkend Lodge overlooks an entrance to the estate, which takes its name from the Norman de Coveston family who first held the manor. Cothelstone House was built as a country residence in 1820 to replace an earlier manorial hall, but whilst the old manor still stands, the 'new' house was demolished in 1968.

Cothelstone, The Beacon Tower 1906 55781
Although not the highest of the Quantock summits, Cothelstone Hill at almost 1,100 feet provides a grand
panorama. The 18th-century builders of the Beacon Tower were not the first to appreciate its qualities, for
Bronze Age peoples buried their dead here. Sad to say, the tower no longer stands, having finally disappeared
around the middle of the 20th century.

Crowcombe, The Village 1929 82120
Seen from the hill, the tower rising behind Glebe House is the oldest part of the Church of the Holy Ghost. It was once topped by a spire, which was struck by lightening in 1725 during an evening service. Although its fall did considerable damage to the church, fortunately none of the congregation was injured.

Crowcombe, The Quantock Gate 1929 82104
From the tiny village of Crowcombe it is a steep climb up a narrow, wooded valley onto the Quantock Hills. The wonderful views have long encouraged recreation, and the poets Samuel Taylor Coleridge and William Wordsworth wandered together up here, 'rapt in fervid talk'. It is said that during one such walk, the outline for 'The Rime of the Ancient Mariner' was planned.

Crowcombe, The Triscombe Stone 1929 82108
High on the hill above the village from which it takes its name lies the Triscombe Stone. Some believe it is a wishing stone, but others warn that the Devil musters his spectral Yeth hounds and horsemen there. They chase across the moors in a frantic hunt and to see or even hear the hounds means certain death.

Wiveliscombe, Court House c1960 W315030 Wiveliscombe has been occupied since the Romans passed by, and during the medieval period it served as a summer residence for the Bishops of Bath and Wells. The Court House is a magnificent Tudor-style building, erected in 1881. Carved wooden panels decorate the corbelled windows and terracotta tiles adorn the façade. Inside, an impressive stairwell rises through the floors.

Taunton Deane and the Blackdown Hills

◄ **Waterrow, The Bridge c1950** W579004
The village was formerly called Skirdal, deriving from a Saxon word meaning a 'clear water dale'; it was only during the 18th century that the hamlet's present name appeared. The building on the left began life some 450 years ago as a smithy and became an inn in the 1850s to service the coach trade. Its name was taken from the rock face against which it is built.

◄ **Wiveliscombe North Street c1955**
W315012
Rendering on the White Hart Hotel has been set within panels, but the decorative emphasis is lost in the application of a uniform colour to the façade. Instead, rows of lights have been added, which, when illuminated at night, no doubt lent prominence to the building. Today, the bulbs have gone and black and white paint achieves the same purpose.

▼ **Halse, The Village c1950** H498501

To the right of the thatched cottages stands the school hall, which has decorated bargeboards and a bell above its gable to call the children to class. Edward Prior, the local squire, built it in 1856. In the wall on the opposite side of the road is a spring, which once supplied the village with its water.

▼ **Bishops Lydeard, Church Street c1960** B868018

Not far from the Church of St Mary the Virgin, crooked cottages line Piffin Lane. The house where father and son sit has since been demolished, and a library now occupies the site. The village's first library was housed in the Lethbridge Arms, to which gentlemen subscribed for the purchase of books that were then lent to the members.

▲ **Bishops Lydeard, Gore Square c1960**
B868012

The pub began life in the 16th century as a cattle drovers' inn, and after the turnpike to Bridgwater was built in 1781, it became an important halt. Originally the Gore Inn, it took its present name from the local landowners of nearby Sandhill Park. The main road now bypasses the town, and the garage opposite no longer sells petrol.

◄ **Taunton,
North Street 1902** 48721
Electric street lighting came
to Taunton in 1886 and was
shortly followed by a public
tramway, whose rails and
overhead cables can be
seen in the photograph.
With no trams in sight,
cyclists appear to favour
the middle of the street,
but are careful not to let
their wheels fall into the
track.

**Taunton,
High Street 1925**
78808
Bullnose Morris
Cowleys were popular
cars of their time, with
a reputation for both
economy and reliability.
The distinctive rounded
radiator made its
appearance in 1913,
but it was to be
replaced in 1927 by a
more 'modern'-looking
flatnose design. Today,
the High Street has
been pedestrianised
and modern shop
fronts disguise the few
buildings that remain
from this period.

**Taunton
The Parade and
North Street 1929**
82090
In June 1685, the
Duke of Monmouth
took Taunton and was
confidently declared
King James II of England
in the High Street.
Barely a month later,
the Parade witnessed
a very different scene,
as prisoners taken at
the Battle of
Sedgemoor were
brought into the square
and thirteen were
summarily hanged as
an example to all.

◀ **Wellington,
South Street c1955**

W45001

Having acquired the estate
here when he was elevated
to the peerage for his
military successes in India
and Europe, the Irish-born
Arthur Wellesley adopted
Wellington for his title.
He went on to gain victory
at Waterloo and became
known as the 'Iron Duke'.
It was he who built the
Town Hall in 1833, from
which this picture was
taken.

◀ Taunton, French Weir 1906

55800

Taken beside what is now Clarence Street, this view looks across the River Tone to St John's Church in the town. Everyone appears dressed in his or her Sunday best, although the day has more of a holiday air. A group of boys try for fish in the river, watched by two young girls, too ladylike to sit on the bank.

▼ Wellington, High Street c1955

W45002

Also taken from the Town Hall, this photograph shows that the main street was less congested than it is today. Yet Wellington has long been a busy and prosperous place, largely owing to its woollen industry. The mills, which lie just outside the town, are owned by the Fox family and are still renowned for producing high quality flannel and material for nurses' uniforms.

◀ Wellington, High Street c1955 W45027

The street is here a little busier, with cars, a bus and several delivery vans parked by the kerb. Loading outside the Co-op is a mobile fish shop. At one time, many areas were served by vans such as these, an effective 'home delivery' service provided by butchers, greengrocers, bakers and others, long before the Internet came along.

Wellington, High Street c1965 W45095
In the 19th century, banking was important to the town with the independent bank of Fox, Fowler and Company having its base here. The company held the distinction of being the last private bank in the country to issue its own notes, and continued in business until it was taken over by Lloyds in 1929.

Rockwell Green, The Post Office c1955 R48303
Now a suburb of Wellington, the village was once known as Rowe Green, but often dubbed 'Rogue Green' because of the unruly behaviour of some of its inhabitants. Near Oaken Ground is an old well, whose waters during the mid 18th century were credited with curative properties, and were regarded particularly beneficial for the treatment of strained and weak eyes.

Around the Southern Hills

Yeovil
High Street 1903   49171
In the 1930s Yeovil was still described as 'an old town', and
this view was typical of its appearance in the early 20th century.
Wartime bombing and town centre redevelopment have changed
its face completely, but some of its architectural heritage has
survived. The ornate bank building on the corner is largely
unchanged, and Denner's continues in business.

Yeovil, Middle Street 1903 49167

At that time, just beyond the heart of the town, the lower end of Middle Street contained a number of comfortable-looking town houses interspersed by occasional shops and businesses. Although its character has since changed and a jumble of shop fronts now lines the street, many of the buildings can still be identified.

Yeovil, The Hospital 1912 64521

A century ago, fresh air and convalescence were accorded the same importance as other elements of the curative process, and many hospital wards led directly onto a veranda. During the day, patients could sit in the sun, which must have been a pleasant experience here, where they overlooked a leafy street, watching the world go by.

Yeovil, The George Hotel 1912 64522
Founded on a low stone wall, this wonderful half-timbered medieval inn once stood in the centre of town on
Middle Street. Its upper story leans out over the street and small leaded panes of glass fill the windows. Short-
sighted 1970s planners demolished it to widen a road that was subsequently pedestrianised, and in its stead built
the town's first supermarket.

Yeovil, Nine Springs 1912 64531A
Just a short walk from the town centre leads to one of Yeovil's beauty spots. A Victorian garden, it was designed around springs bubbling from the hillside, which were channelled into a series of waterfalls and ponds. A network of woodland paths still provides a pleasant stroll, but this pretty thatched cottage, which once served afternoon teas, has now disappeared.

Barwick, The House and Gardens 1900 45327
This ornate house lies two miles south of Yeovil and was built by the Newmans in the 18th century. A nearby folly, known as 'Jack the Treacle Eater', represents a foot-messenger employed by Messiters, a Wincanton banking family, who subsequently inherited the house. Jack supposedly ran back and forth to London on a diet of bread and treacle.

East Coker, The Almshouses c1955 E238016
The Helvars, who then owned nearby Coker Court, erected these almshouses in 1640. Shortly after their construction, the village's most famous son was born, William Dampier. Going to sea at 16, he achieved fame and notoriety as both an explorer and buccaneer; amongst his exploits, he is remembered for having circumnavigated the globe three times.

Brympton, The House 1900 45328
Behind a lichen-covered balustrade stands Brympton House, little changed in a century. Replacing an earlier house, which still stands nearby, it was built by the Sydenhams in the early 16th century and claims the largest single span staircase in the country. The small chapel has an unusual belfry, and contains monuments to successive generations of the families holding the manor.

Brympton, The House and the Lake 1900 45502
The south façade of the house is built in the 17th-century English Renaissance style, with pedimented bays overlooking a terrace and lawn to a lake below. In 1722, Francis Fane of Bristol bought the house; his descendants restored and opened it to visitors during the 1970s and 80s. It has since been sold again, and is now closed to the public.

Montacute, The Church and the Priory c1960 M92016
The gatehouse, standing left of centre, is all that remains of a late 11th-century Cluniac priory. It was founded beneath St Michael's Hill, which was regarded a sacred place after a flint cross was found buried there in 1035. The parish church of St Catherine grew out of a chapel that stood in the monks' burial ground.

Tintinhull, The Green c1955 T345003
The shade of an old lime tree at the foot of the village green provides an excellent spot for this family's picnic. The scene is little changed today, although the young tree in the foreground has grown to maturity and milk churns no longer wait beside the road for collection by the dairy.

◀ Ilchester
The Cross Roads c1965
175022

The market cross is an imposing structure, reflecting Ilchester's former status as the county town. Surmounted by four sundials and a weathervane, it was erected in 1795 over the original medieval cross for the princely sum of £35 10s 3¾d. However, after being blown down in a storm, the cost of its rebuilding in 1991 was over £17,000.

Tintinhull, The Stocks c1955 T345026

At one time, almost every town and village had its stocks, which in some places continued in use as a means of public humiliation and punishment into the Victorian era. When the tree behind these became unsafe and subsequently taken down, the stocks were re-moved, but copies were sold in the village to raise money for charity.

Ilchester, Yeovil Road c1955 I75007

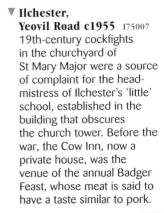

19th-century cockfights in the churchyard of St Mary Major were a source of complaint for the head-mistress of Ilchester's 'little' school, established in the building that obscures the church tower. Before the war, the Cow Inn, now a private house, was the venue of the annual Badger Feast, whose meat is said to have a taste similar to pork.

Ilchester The Ilchester Hotel c1965 I75020

Originally the Swan, the hotel is here called the Ivelchester, the town's name until the 1930s, which derives from the Saxon 'Givelcestreand', describing a Roman camp on the River Givel. 'Ilchester' evolved on the tongues of servicemen stationed nearby during the last war, but the old name survived in the hotel until it was 'modernised' quite recently by a transient landlord.

▼ Martock, The Market House and the Pinnacle c1950 M42007

The Market Hall bears an advertisement for the White Hart, which lies around the corner. When it was built in 1750, the open arcading on the ground floor contained the butcher's shambles and also provided a home for the town's fire cart. The upper story served for parochial meetings, and is still a venue for the Parish Council.

▼ Martock, East Street c1955 M42008

Known as the Pinnacle, the market cross was also erected in 1750, but its recent history is marred by accident, having twice been demolished by lorries since the 1970s. At the back stands the 13th-century Church of All Saints, which was built as an abbey church subordinate to the French monastery at le Mont-St-Michel.

▲ South Petherton, St James Street c1960
S412003

Along the street on the right is Blake Hall, erected for the 'furtherance of the Liberal cause' to the memory of William Blake in 1911. Rising above thatched roofs is the church of St Peter and St Paul. Culminating in a spire, its Early English octagonal tower is said to be the highest of its type in the country.

◄ **Barrington,
The Chapel and the
Church c1960** B822008
Octagonal towers, such as
the one above St Mary's,
are a feature of many
churches in this part of
Somerset. Close by, on
the right, stands a
Wesleyan chapel.
During the 18th century,
many working-class people
turned to non-conformist
movements, rejecting the
established church for its
pious attitude and the
irrelevance of its preaching
to their often hand-to-
mouth existence.

Shepton Beauchamp, The Shambles c1955 S787007

In the 14th century, the manor became the property of the Seymours from Normandy, a descendent of whom became Henry VIII's third wife. Jane had been lady-in-waiting to both Catherine of Aragon and Anne Boleyn, and within days of Anne's execution was married to the King. She died the following year, bearing the future Edward VI.

Hinton St George, The Cross c1955 H513010

Although much worn by the passage of time, the figure of St John the Baptist is still recognisable on the village's 15th-century cross. The cottages behind were demolished following a fire in the 1960s. A similar disaster more recently hit another cottage lower down, opposite the shop; however, extensive repairs have restored its former appearance.

Hinton St George, The Post Office and the Cross c1955 H513014
Seen here is the village shop and post office whilst opposite, outside the farm, milk churns await collection. The nearby church contains several impressive funerary monuments of the Poulett family, who acquired the manor by marriage in the 15th century. Amyas, the first of the family born here, is remembered for committing a drunken young Cardinal Wolsey to the stocks.

Haselbury Plucknett, The Stores c1955 H393003
Although the window might be Spartan, no shortage of signs advertise the shop's presence. The nearby church was founded above the cell of a 12th-century hermit, Wulfric, who renounced his noble birth and wore chain-mail in penance. Known for his wisdom, he divined Stephen's accession to the throne, and after his death, his grave became a focus for pilgrimage.

▼ **Crewkerne, The View from the Church Tower c1955** C185003
Looking west from the top of St Bartholomew's tower, the view across the countryside has changed little over the years, and might still be recognised by Thomas Hardy, who served as a captain under Nelson. He attended the town's grammar school, which in those days was housed in the adjacent Jacobean church hall.

▼ **Crewkerne, Market Square c1950** C185019
The balconied building overlooking the square was built in the 18th century as the town's market, but its once-open ground floor was remodelled by the Victorians and enclosed. Opposite, but out of view, the George Hotel is a former coaching inn, whose 17th-century owner, Thomas Hutchin, was also postmaster and introduced a postal service between London and Plymouth.

▲ **Crewkerne, Market Street c1955**
C185034
Crewkerne's prosperity in the 18th century derived from a flourishing flax industry, which employed almost a quarter of the population and produced the sailcloth for Nelson's flagship. That wealth is reflected in a legacy of fine Georgian buildings; although many here in the town's main shopping street have been altered to accommodate shops, their upper stories remain largely unaffected.

◄ **Chard, The Old Toll House 1940**
C58009
West of the town at the top of
Snowdon Hill is the Old Toll House,
built of local stone and flint and
still possessing a thatched over-
hanging roof that is supported on
wooden posts. The main A30 road
now passes around the other side
of the building, to follow a less
sinuous course over the hill to
Yarcombe.

**Chard,
Cottages 1907** 58768
At the beginning of the
20th century, the town
was more compact than
it is today, and these
cottages, which can
still be found on the
northern edge of
the town, were very
much part of a rural
community. The
bearded farmer leading
the two working horses
has perhaps come from
the farm that lay behind
the thatched cottages.

Chard, Fore Street 1907 58760
The town climbs along the length of a wide main street, which is thought to follow the line of a Roman road. Mitchell and Toms, whose name adorns the elaborately decorated, but now sadly demolished, building on the right, were brewers and distillers. Their business continued in the town until it was taken over by Charringtons in the 1960s.

Chard, Fore Street c1955 C58026
Right of the Westminster Bank stands Manor Court, which was built as a merchant's house in 1550; in the upper rooms, some ceilings still retain their fine plasterwork decoration. Just distinguishable by its tall chimneys at the top of the street is Harvey's Hospital. Rebuilt in 1841, it was bequeathed to the town's poor by a 17th-century merchant.

Chard, The Guildhall 1907 58765
Two tiers of Tuscan pillars form an impressive portico and balcony at the front of the Guildhall, which
was built around 1835 to serve as a market with the town hall above. It also housed the town's
prison. The importance of agriculture in the surrounding area is reflected in its extension, some fifty
years later, to accommodate a corn exchange.

▼ Chard, High Street and Cornhill c1960 C58050

One of High Street's more famous residents was John Stringfellow, who was apprenticed here in the lace industry at the beginning of the 19th century. He subsequently followed his father's trade as an engineer and, after an initial collaboration with William Henson, he designed a steam powered model aircraft that flew for 120 feet.

▼ Chard, Fore Street c1965 C58071

A plaque on the Guildhall remembers another of Chard's famous people, Margaret Grace Bondfield. A lace worker's daughter, she entered politics through an involvement in trade unionism and was elected member for Northampton in 1923. She became chairman of the TUC and later was the first woman cabinet member, serving as Minister of Labour between 1929 and 1931.

▲ Ilminster, West Street 1907 58742

A horse trap was still a common sight in the early 20th century, and the people outside the shops are more interested in the photographer at work. Samways provision store has gone, demolished to widen the road, but the Ilminster Fish Supply continues to sell fish, although now parcelled in batter and accompanied by chips.

◀ **Ilminster,
Market Square 1907**

58746

Overlooking the Market Square at the bottom of North Street is the George Hotel, the first hotel in which Queen Victoria stayed, in 1819 - she was just seven months old. In 1685, the square was the scene of a more gruesome event, when Charles Speke was hanged in lieu of his brother John, who had been a leader in Monmouth's rebel army.

Ilminster, New Road 1907 58748
Rising above West Street, these houses were only some twenty years old when this photograph was taken. Built in undressed local stone, the surrounds to the doors and windows are attractively decorated in contrasting brick and terracotta work. Further ornament is given by carved bargeboards on the gables and the corbels which support canopies over the doors and bay windows.

Ilminster, Silver Street c1950 17018
St Mary's Church, which rises behind the Dolphin Hotel, is renowned for its lavishly-decorated tower and impressive tie beam roof, both of which date from its rebuilding in the 15th century. Sir William Wadham, whose family also founded the town's grammar school and Wadham College at Oxford in 1612, financed much of the work.

Ilminster, Court Barton 1907 58750
Off Court Barton, opposite the church, stand chantry houses where a boys' grammar school was founded in 1549. In the 19th century, it was moved to other premises to make way for a grammar school for girls. The building graced with an imposing classical porch is Cross House, which was once the headmaster's residence.

◀ **Bridgwater,
Eastover c1950** B205031
Medieval Bridgwater grew
prosperous from wool and
trade to become a major
port. In the 20th century
a variety of industries
developed, including the
manufacture of bricks, tiles,
shirts and Cellophane.
This view shows one of the
town's once busy shopping
streets, but subsequent redevelopment has concen-
trated the main retail outlets
on the western side of the
river.

The Somerset Levels

◀ **Cannington,
The Village c1965**
C733020
Two bridges and a ford
cross the stream that flows
past the Blue Anchor Inn,
which stands at the centre
of the village. A pub since
at least 1870, it was largely
rebuilt in 1947 and
renamed the 'Friendly
Spirit' about seventeen
years ago on account of an
inoffensive ghost said to
appear in one of the upper
rooms.

◀ **Bridgwater, The Bridge 1903**
50451
The main port lay north of this
point, since a medieval three-
arched stone bridge blocked the
further passage of tall craft
upstream along the River Parrett;
even in the early 20th century,
sailing boats still moored at the
quayside. The wrought and cast
iron span shown here was
opened in 1883 and still carries
traffic into the town centre.

Bridgwater, The River 1927 80592

Beyond the port's wharves, the Parrett's banks remained undeveloped, and tree-lined roads along the river's edge from the town made a pleasant promenade. The infirmary, overlooking the river to the right of the photograph, was financed by voluntary contributions, whilst much of the £3,500 needed for the library on the opposite bank came from the Carnegie Trust.

Bridgwater, The YMCA 1890 27897

Although several of the buildings along the riverfront have survived the town's redevelopment schemes, this one was demolished in the 1960s. The YMCA, now an international organisation, was founded in 1844 by George Williams, its objectives being to encourage spiritual, intellectual and physical self-improvement. Women members have been accepted since 1971.

Bridgwater, The Market House 1897 40000

At the top of Fore Street is the main square, which is presided over by the elegant classical architecture of the Corn Exchange and Market Hall, built around 1834. Behind rises the slender octagonal spire of St Mary's Church, which was built in the early 15th century and is 174 feet high.

◀ **Bridgwater,
The Royal Clarence Hotel
1890** 27901
In the 1930s it cost around 15 shillings a day to stay at the Clarence, which was once the main hotel in the town. Although the building remains today, it is no longer a hotel, and perhaps it is ironic that Taylor's High Street Restaurant now trades as a fast food outlet.

Bridgwater, Blake's House 1906 55771
The town's most celebrated son, Robert Blake, was born here in 1598. MP for Bridgwater in 1640, he gave strong support to Cromwell's cause and demonstrated his military abilities during the successful defence of Taunton against overwhelming Royalist forces. Blake was subsequently given command of the Navy, a position he held for nine years.

Westonzoyland, Sedgemoor Battlefield c1960 W603303
This monument was erected in 1928 at the site of Monmouth's defeat at the hands of the Royalist army in memory of all those killed during the battle or who subsequently suffered imprisonment, transportation or execution for their support of Monmouth's cause. The four 'mushrooms' are century stones, inscribed with the major British battles of the last four hundred years.

High Ham, The Village Green c1965 H508003
Looking across the village green, this view has changed little during the last forty years. To the right of the photograph stands St Andrew's Church, rebuilt during the 15th century by the monks of Glastonbury, to whom the manor belonged from the middle of the 10th century until the Dissolution.

High Ham, The Village c1965 H508010
The King's Head still stands beside the road, which drops north from the village to the moors below. A cottage on the left was once home to the blacksmith; his forge stood beyond the pub. The cottages were demolished shortly after this photograph was taken and have since been replaced by modern bungalows.

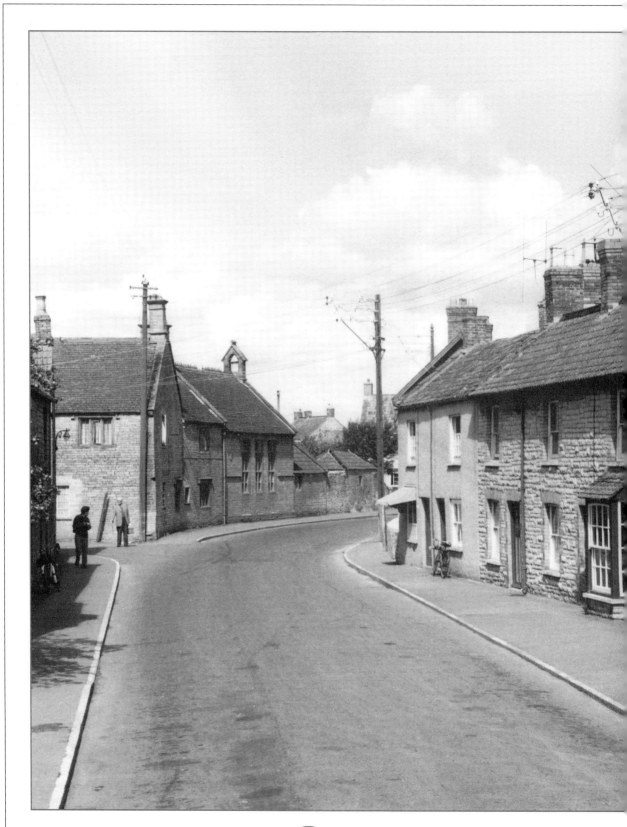

**Somerton,
Langport Road c1960**
S147048
Once the county town
and seat of justice,
Somerton remains
an impressive and
attractive place. Its
streets are lined with
an assortment of stone
buildings, where the
styles of different ages
blend harmoniously.
The hardware store
shown here displays
the wide assortment
of goods once
stocked by local shops,
offering a service and
convenience often hard
to come by today.

◄ **Somerton,
The Viaduct c1955**
S147031
Looking from the B3153, just east of the town, this photograph shows a local train hauled by a steam engine, whilst the cows below, well used to the noise, continue unconcernedly chewing the cud. The track is the main line between Paddington and Exeter, and here is carried above the River Carey on the back of a five-arch viaduct.

Somerton, The Coronation Fountain 1904

52502

People stand conversing by the Coronation Fountain, which was erected in 1902 to commemorate King Edward VII's accession to the throne. It is an ornate affair, decorated with lions' heads and winged sphinxes; fitted with troughs and basins, it provided refreshment for people, horses and dogs. Behind is the Old Hall and to the left, St Michael's Church.

Somerton, The Court 1906 52515

Standing on what was once a Roman site, the first manor house was erected in 1176 by William de Erleigh, whose family remained in possession for some 350 years. Perhaps its most famous occupant was Edward IV's brother, the Duke of Clarence, who drowned in a vat of malmsey. Somerton Court is now a hotel and reception venue.

Burrow Bridge, The Village c1955

B839009

This hamlet was once a port on the River Parrett and the only crossing point between Bridgwater and Langport. The first bridge, erected about the 14th century, served until the present bridge was constructed in 1826. Just visible behind the trees is a ruined tower on top of the Mump, all that remains of a 13th-century church.

Langport, The Hanging Chapel c1955 L365034
Built for a medieval trade guild, this curious building, carried on an arch above the road, has served many purposes in its time, including a school and town hall and is now a Masonic lodge. The cottage on the right housed Langport's second police station and was used as such between about 1920 and the 1960s.

Langport, The Hill c1955 L365015
Many of the town's elegant buildings were built during the 18th century, when the town prospered from the East Indies trade. Goods were carried on river barges between the busy seaport of Bridgwater and wharves here, and one of the entrepreneurs, George Stuckley, also ran a successful bank, which remained independent until taken over by the Westminster in 1909.

Muchelney, The Abbey c1965 M387080
Possibly founded around 720 by King Ine, soon after Glastonbury was founded, Muchelney grew into a small but relatively wealthy community. Abandoned at the Dissolution, only the foundations of its great church remain, but the abbot's lodgings continued in secular use as a house until 1927. To the left is the reredorter or monks' latrine, all now preserved by English Heritage.

Muchelney, The Monks' Reredorter c1965 M387067
Isolated on an island amidst the marshes, the community grew lax and neglected their religious discipline; the monks developed a taste for worldly comforts. When the bishop of Bath and Wells visited in the early 14th century, he was not impressed with their conduct and commanded them to build the nearby parish church and provide it with a priest.

Curry Rivel, Fore Street c1955 C734008
The villagers once derived their living by cutting
osiers to weave baskets, but although none are
displayed here in Jackson's hardware store, the
shop seems to supply most other household
requirements, including oil. In the 1950s central
heating was rare, and many people relied on
paraffin oil heaters to keep their houses warm.

Index

Frith Book Co Titles

www.francisfrith.co.uk

The Frith Book Company publishes over 100 new titles each year. A selection of those currently available are listed below. For latest catalogue please contact Frith Book Co.

Town Books 96 pages, approx 100 photos. County and Themed Books 128 pages, approx 150 photos (unless specified). All titles hardback laminated case and jacket except those indicated pb (paperback)

Title	ISBN	Price	Title	ISBN	Price
Amersham, Chesham & Rickmansworth (pb)			Derby (pb)	1-85937-367-4	£9.99
	1-85937-340-2	£9.99	Derbyshire (pb)	1-85937-196-5	£9.99
Ancient Monuments & Stone Circles	1-85937-143-4	£17.99	Devon (pb)	1-85937-297-x	£9.99
Aylesbury (pb)	1-85937-227-9	£9.99	Dorset (pb)	1-85937-269-4	£9.99
Bakewell	1-85937-113-2	£12.99	Dorset Churches	1-85937-172-8	£17.99
Barnstaple (pb)	1-85937-300-3	£9.99	Dorset Coast (pb)	1-85937-299-6	£9.99
Bath (pb)	1-85937419-0	£9.99	Dorset Living Memories	1-85937-210-4	£14.99
Bedford (pb)	1-85937-205-8	£9.99	Down the Severn	1-85937-118-3	£14.99
Berkshire (pb)	1-85937-191-4	£9.99	Down the Thames (pb)	1-85937-278-3	£9.99
Berkshire Churches	1-85937-170-1	£17.99	Down the Trent	1-85937-311-9	£14.99
Blackpool (pb)	1-85937-382-8	£9.99	Dublin (ph)	1-85937-231-7	£9.99
Bognor Regis (pb)	1-85937-431-x	£9.99	East Anglia (pb)	1-85937-265-1	£9.99
Bournemouth	1-85937-067-5	£12.99	East London	1-85937-080-2	£14.99
Bradford (pb)	1-85937-204-x	£9.99	East Sussex	1-85937-130-2	£14.99
Brighton & Hove(pb)	1-85937-192-2	£8.99	Eastbourne	1-85937-061-6	£12.99
Bristol (pb)	1-85937-264-3	£9.99	Edinburgh (pb)	1-85937-193-0	£8.99
British Life A Century Ago (pb)	1-85937-213-9	£9.99	England in the 1880s	1-85937-331-3	£17.99
Buckinghamshire (pb)	1-85937-200-7	£9.99	English Castles (pb)	1-85937-434-4	£9.99
Camberley (pb)	1-85937-222-8	£9.99	English Country Houses	1-85937-161-2	£17.99
Cambridge (pb)	1-85937-422-0	£9.99	Essex (pb)	1-85937-270-8	£9.99
Cambridgeshire (pb)	1-85937-420-4	£9.99	Exeter	1-85937-126-4	£12.99
Canals & Waterways (pb)	1-85937-291-0	£9.99	Exmoor	1-85937-132-9	£14.99
Canterbury Cathedral (pb)	1-85937-179-5	£9.99	Falmouth	1-85937-066-7	£12.99
Cardiff (pb)	1-85937-093-4	£9.99	Folkestone (pb)	1-85937-124-8	£9.99
Carmarthenshire	1-85937-216-3	£14.99	Glasgow (pb)	1-85937-190-6	£9.99
Chelmsford (pb)	1-85937-310-0	£9.99	Gloucestershire	1-85937-102-7	£14.99
Cheltenham (pb)	1-85937-095-0	£9.99	Great Yarmouth (pb)	1-85937-426-3	£9.99
Cheshire (pb)	1-85937-271-6	£9.99	Greater Manchester (pb)	1-85937-266-x	£9.99
Chester	1-85937-090-x	£12.99	Guildford (pb)	1-85937-410-7	£9.99
Chesterfield	1-85937-378-x	£9.99	Hampshire (pb)	1-85937-279-1	£9.99
Chichester (pb)	1-85937-228-7	£9.99	Hampshire Churches (pb)	1-85937-207-4	£9.99
Colchester (pb)	1-85937-188-4	£8.99	Harrogate	1-85937-423-9	£9.99
Cornish Coast	1-85937-163-9	£14.99	Hastings & Bexhill (pb)	1-85937-131-0	£9.99
Cornwall (pb)	1-85937-229-5	£9.99	Heart of Lancashire (pb)	1-85937-197-3	£9.99
Cornwall Living Memories	1-85937-248-1	£14.99	Helston (pb)	1-85937-214-7	£9.99
Cotswolds (pb)	1-85937-230-9	£9.99	Hereford (pb)	1-85937-175-2	£9.99
Cotswolds Living Memories	1-85937-255-4	£14.99	Herefordshire	1-85937-174-4	£14.99
County Durham	1-85937-123-x	£14.99	Hertfordshire (pb)	1-85937-247-3	£9.99
Croydon Living Memories	1-85937-162-0	£9.99	Horsham (pb)	1-85937-432-8	£9.99
Cumbria	1-85937-101-9	£14.99	Humberside	1-85937-215-5	£14.99
Dartmoor	1-85937-145-0	£14.99	Hythe, Romney Marsh & Ashford	1-85937-256-2	£9.99

Available from your local bookshop or from the publisher

Frith Book Co Titles (continued)

Ipswich (pb)	1-85937-424-7	£9.99	St Ives (pb)	1-85937415-8	£9.99
Ireland (pb)	1-85937-181-7	£9.99	Scotland (pb)	1-85937-182-5	£9.99
Isle of Man (pb)	1-85937-268-6	£9.99	Scottish Castles (pb)	1-85937-323-2	£9.99
Isles of Scilly	1-85937-136-1	£14.99	Sevenoaks & Tunbridge	1-85937-057-8	£12.99
Isle of Wight (pb)	1-85937-429-8	£9.99	Sheffield, South Yorks (pb)	1-85937-267-8	£9.99
Isle of Wight Living Memories	1-85937-304-6	£14.99	Shrewsbury (pb)	1-85937-325-9	£9.99
Kent (pb)	1-85937-189-2	£9.99	Shropshire (pb)	1-85937-326-7	£9.99
Kent Living Memories	1-85937-125-6	£14.99	Somerset	1-85937-153-1	£14.99
Lake District (pb)	1-85937-275-9	£9.99	South Devon Coast	1-85937-107-8	£14.99
Lancaster, Morecambe & Heysham (pb)	1-85937-233-3	£9.99	South Devon Living Memories	1-85937-168-x	£14.99
Leeds (pb)	1-85937-202-3	£9.99	South Hams	1-85937-220-1	£14.99
Leicester	1-85937-073-x	£12.99	Southampton (pb)	1-85937-427-1	£9.99
Leicestershire (pb)	1-85937-185-x	£9.99	Southport (pb)	1-85937-425-5	£9.99
Lincolnshire (pb)	1-85937-433-6	£9.99	Staffordshire	1-85937-047-0	£12.99
Liverpool & Merseyside (pb)	1-85937-234-1	£9.99	Stratford upon Avon	1-85937-098-5	£12.99
London (pb)	1-85937-183-3	£9.99	Suffolk (pb)	1-85937-221-x	£9.99
Ludlow (pb)	1-85937-176-0	£9.99	Suffolk Coast	1-85937-259-7	£14.99
Luton (pb)	1-85937-235-x	£9.99	Surrey (pb)	1-85937-240-6	£9.99
Maidstone	1-85937-056-x	£14.99	Sussex (pb)	1-85937-184-1	£9.99
Manchester (pb)	1-85937-198-1	£9.99	Swansea (pb)	1-85937-167-1	£9.99
Middlesex	1-85937-158-2	£14.99	Tees Valley & Cleveland	1-85937-211-2	£14.99
New Forest	1-85937-128-0	£14.99	Thanet (pb)	1-85937-116-7	£9.99
Newark (pb)	1-85937-366-6	£9.99	Tiverton (pb)	1-85937-178-7	£9.99
Newport, Wales (pb)	1-85937-258-9	£9.99	Torbay	1-85937-063-2	£12.99
Newquay (pb)	1-85937-421-2	£9.99	Truro	1-85937-147-7	£12.99
Norfolk (pb)	1-85937-195-7	£9.99	Victorian and Edwardian Cornwall	1-85937-252-x	£14.99
Norfolk Living Memories	1-85937-217-1	£14.99	Victorian & Edwardian Devon	1-85937-253-8	£14.99
Northamptonshire	1-85937-150-7	£14.99	Victorian & Edwardian Kent	1-85937-149-3	£14.99
Northumberland Tyne & Wear (pb)	1-85937-281-3	£9.99	Vic & Ed Maritime Album	1-85937-144-2	£17.99
North Devon Coast	1-85937-146-9	£14.99	Victorian and Edwardian Sussex	1-85937-157-4	£14.99
North Devon Living Memories	1-85937-261-9	£14.99	Victorian & Edwardian Yorkshire	1-85937-154-x	£14.99
North London	1-85937-206-6	£14.99	Victorian Seaside	1-85937-159-0	£17.99
North Wales (pb)	1-85937-298-8	£9.99	Villages of Devon (pb)	1-85937-293-7	£9.99
North Yorkshire (pb)	1-85937-236-8	£9.99	Villages of Kent (pb)	1-85937-294-5	£9.99
Norwich (pb)	1-85937-194-9	£8.99	Villages of Sussex (pb)	1-85937-295-3	£9.99
Nottingham (pb)	1-85937-324-0	£9.99	Warwickshire (pb)	1-85937-203-1	£9.99
Nottinghamshire (pb)	1-85937-187-6	£9.99	Welsh Castles (pb)	1-85937-322-4	£9.99
Oxford (pb)	1-85937-411-5	£9.99	West Midlands (pb)	1-85937-289-9	£9.99
Oxfordshire (pb)	1-85937-430-1	£9.99	West Sussex	1-85937-148-5	£14.99
Peak District (pb)	1-85937-280-5	£9.99	West Yorkshire (pb)	1-85937-201-5	£9.99
Penzance	1-85937-069-1	£12.99	Weymouth (pb)	1-85937-209-0	£9.99
Peterborough (pb)	1-85937-219-8	£9.99	Wiltshire (pb)	1-85937-277-5	£9.99
Piers	1-85937-237-6	£17.99	Wiltshire Churches (pb)	1-85937-171-x	£9.99
Plymouth	1-85937-119-1	£12.99	Wiltshire Living Memories	1-85937-245-7	£14.99
Poole & Sandbanks (pb)	1-85937-251-1	£9.99	Winchester (pb)	1-85937-428-x	£9.99
Preston (pb)	1-85937-212-0	£9.99	Windmills & Watermills	1-85937-242-2	£17.99
Reading (pb)	1-85937-238-4	£9.99	Worcester (pb)	1-85937-165-5	£9.99
Romford (pb)	1-85937-319-4	£9.99	Worcestershire	1-85937-152-3	£14.99
Salisbury (pb)	1-85937-239-2	£9.99	York (pb)	1-85937-199-x	£9.99
Scarborough (pb)	1-85937-379-8	£9.99	Yorkshire (pb)	1-85937-186-8	£9.99
St Albans (pb)	1-85937-341-0	£9.99	Yorkshire Living Memories	1-85937-166-3	£14.99

See Frith books on the internet www.francisfrith.co.uk

FRITH PRODUCTS & SERVICES

Francis Frith would doubtless be pleased to know that the pioneering publishing venture he started in 1860 still continues today. A hundred and forty years later, The Francis Frith Collection continues in the same innovative tradition and is now one of the foremost publishers of vintage photographs in the world. Some of the current activities include:

Interior Decoration

Today Frith's photographs can be seen framed and as giant wall murals in thousands of pubs, restaurants, hotels, banks, retail stores and other public buildings throughout the country. In every case they enhance the unique local atmosphere of the places they depict and provide reminders of gentler days in an increasingly busy and frenetic world.

Product Promotions

Frith products are used by many major companies to promote the sales of their own products or to reinforce their own history and heritage. Frith promotions have been used by Hovis bread, Courage beers, Scots Porage Oats, Colman's mustard, Cadbury's foods, Mellow Birds coffee, Dunhill pipe tobacco, Guinness, and Bulmer's Cider.

Genealogy and Family History

As the interest in family history and roots grows world-wide, more and more people are turning to Frith's photographs of Great Britain for images of the towns, villages and streets where their ancestors lived; and, of course, photographs of the churches and chapels where their ancestors were christened, married and buried are an essential part of every genealogy tree and family album.

Frith Products

All Frith photographs are available Framed or just as Mounted Prints and Posters (size 23 x 16 inches). These may be ordered from the address below. From time to time other products - Address Books, Calendars, Table Mats, etc - are available.

The Internet

Already twenty thousand Frith photographs can be viewed and purchased on the internet through the Frith websites and a myriad of partner sites.

For more detailed information on Frith companies and products, look at these sites:

www.francisfrith.co.uk
www.francisfrith.com
(for North American visitors)

See the complete list of Frith Books at:

www.francisfrith.co.uk

This web site is regularly updated with the latest list of publications from the Frith Book Company. If you wish to buy books relating to another part of the country that your local bookshop does not stock, you may purchase on-line.

For further information, trade, or author enquiries please contact us at the address below:
The Francis Frith Collection, Frith's Barn, Teffont, Salisbury, Wiltshire, England SP3 5QP.
Tel: +44 (0)1722 716 376 Fax: +44 (0)1722 716 881 Email: sales@francisfrith.co.uk

See Frith books on the internet www.francisfrith.co.uk

TO RECEIVE YOUR FREE MOUNTED PRINT

Mounted Print
Overall size 14 x 11 inches

Cut out this Voucher and return it with your remittance for £1.95 to cover postage and handling, to UK addresses. For overseas addresses please include £4.00 post and handling. Choose any photograph included in this book. Your SEPIA print will be A4 in size, and mounted in a cream mount with burgundy rule line, overall size 14 x 11 inches.

Order additional Mounted Prints at HALF PRICE (only £7.49 each*)

If there are further pictures you would like to order, possibly as gifts for friends and family, purchase them at half price (no additional postage and handling required).

Have your Mounted Prints framed*

For an additional £14.95 per print you can have your chosen Mounted Print framed in an elegant polished wood and gilt moulding, overall size 16 x 13 inches (no additional postage and handling required).

---

* IMPORTANT!
These special prices are only available if ordered using the original voucher on this page (no copies permitted) and at the same time as your free Mounted Print, for delivery to the same address

---

Frith Collectors' Guild

From time to time we publish a magazine of news and stories about Frith photographs and further special offers of Frith products. If you would like 12 months FREE membership, please return this form.

Send completed forms to:
**The Francis Frith Collection,
Frith's Barn, Teffont, Salisbury,
Wiltshire SP3 5QP**

Voucher for FREE and Reduced Price Frith Prints

Picture no.	Page number	Qty	Mounted @ £7.49	Framed + £14.95	Total Cost
		1	**Free of charge***	£	£
			£7.49	£	£
			£7.49	£	£
			£7.49	£	£
			£7.49	£	£
			£7.49	£	£

Please allow 28 days for delivery	*** Post & handling**	**£1.95**
Book Title	**Total Order Cost**	**£**

Please do not photocopy this voucher. Only the original is valid, so please cut it out and return it to us.

I enclose a cheque / postal order for £ . . . .
made payable to 'The Francis Frith Collection'
OR please debit my Mastercard / Visa / Switch / Amex card
(credit cards please on all overseas orders)

Number . . . .

Issue No(Switch only) . . . . .Valid from (Amex/Switch) . . . .

Expires . . . . Signature . . . .

Name Mr/Mrs/Ms . . . .

Address . . . .

. . . .

. . . . Postcode . . . .

Daytime Tel No . . . .   Valid to 31/12/02

The Francis Frith Collectors' Guild

Please enrol me as a member for 12 months free of charge.

Name Mr/Mrs/Ms . . . .

Address . . . .

. . . .

. . . . Postcode . . . .

Would you like to find out more about Francis Frith?

We have recently recruited some entertaining speakers who are happy to visit local groups, clubs and societies to give an illustrated talk documenting Frith's travels and photographs. If you are a member of such a group and are interested in hosting a presentation, we would love to hear from you.

Our speakers bring with them a small selection of our local town and county books, together with sample prints. They are happy to take orders. A small proportion of the order value is donated to the group who have hosted the presentation. The talks are therefore an excellent way of fundraising for small groups and societies.

Can you help us with information about any of the Frith photographs in this book?

We are gradually compiling an historical record for each of the photographs in the Frith archive. It is always fascinating to find out the names of the people shown in the pictures, as well as insights into the shops, buildings and other features depicted.

If you recognize anyone in the photographs in this book, or if you have information not already included in the author's caption, do let us know. We would love to hear from you, and will try to publish it in future books or articles.

Our production team

Frith books are produced by a small dedicated team at offices in the converted Grade II listed 18th-century barn at Teffont near Salisbury, illustrated above. Most have worked with the Frith Collection for many years. All have in common one quality: they have a passion for the Frith Collection. The team is constantly expanding, but currently includes:

Jason Buck, John Buck, Douglas Burns, Heather Crisp, Isobel Hall, Rob Hames, Hazel Heaton, Peter Horne, James Kinnear, Tina Leary, Hannah Marsh, Eliza Sackett, Terence Sackett, Sandra Sanger, Shelley Tolcher, Susanna Walker, Clive Wathen and Jenny Wathen.